Other Works by Nancy Sanks

Finding Balance in Uncertain Times; One day workshop

Finding Balance: The Course; Six week program

Eastern Wisdom and Western Lifestyle; One day workshop

Tools for Ageless Living with Yoga and
Ayurveda; One day workshop

Body Awareness Yoga Retreats 1-3 days

Body Awareness and Conscious Living;
Six week personal program

All the above are described on the website:
www.bodyawarenessyoga.com

FINDING BALANCE
IN UNCERTAIN TIMES
LIFE LINES TO INNER PEACE

NANCY J. SANKS

BALBOA.PRESS
A DIVISION OF HAY HOUSE

Balboa Press books may be ordered through booksellers or by contacting:

Balboa Press
A Division of Hay House
1663 Liberty Drive
Bloomington, IN 47403
www.balboapress.com
1 (877) 407-4847

Because of the dynamic nature of the Internet, any web addresses or
links contained in this book may have changed since publication and
may no longer be valid. The views expressed in this work are solely those
of the author and do not necessarily reflect the views of the publisher,
and the publisher hereby disclaims any responsibility for them.

The author of this book does not dispense medical advice or prescribe the use
of any technique as a form of treatment for physical, emotional, or medical
problems without the advice of a physician, either directly or indirectly. The
intent of the author is only to offer information of a general nature to help
you in your quest for emotional and spiritual well-being. In the event you use
any of the information in this book for yourself, which is your constitutional
right, the author and the publisher assume no responsibility for your actions.

Any people depicted in stock imagery provided by Getty Images are
models, and such images are being used for illustrative purposes only.
Certain stock imagery © Getty Images.

Print information available on the last page.

ISBN: 978-1-9822-5101-7 (sc)
ISBN: 978-1-9822-5102-4 (e)

Library of Congress Control Number: 2020913057

Balboa Press rev. date: 07/31/2020

This book is dedicated to my students, family, friends and all who are looking for balance in these uncertain times

CONTENTS

INTRODUCTION

E very new season in our life announces itself through difficulty, confusion, or a sense of being uprooted. To navigate this change we must find our inner resource, an anchor that can be used to maintain connection to "self" while being fully present and available to what is happening *now.*

Over the past four decades I have been involved in the wellness world, including Yoga and Ayurveda. These two life sciences have offered me ways to integrate family and daily life lessons into my spiritual practice. They are the teachings I share to help others creatively problem solve and gain more peace in their lives.

Body Awareness Yoga was founded in 1989 after completing my first yoga teacher training. Since then, I've continued to study with master teachers from various traditions and cultures around the world. It is with humble gratitude to these mentors and Kripalu Center for Yoga and Health, that I share these teachings with you.

In this book (designed as a resource for the workshop) we will explore ways to move forward in the midst of turmoil. Using breath work (pranayama), movement and poses (asana), and mindfulness (meditation), we can find a path to physical, mental, and spiritual balance.

Each lifeline in this book provides the reader with an opportunity to engage physically, mentally, and spiritually to the concepts and practices outlined within the chapter. Each chapter includes several practices to choose from and offers encouragement through stories shared by those who have taken this journey and used the practices to manage their challenges.

Our first lifeline to finding balance is the **breath**: Our constant companion from birth to death. It is witness to our entire life - the good, the bad, the ugly, the beauty, the joy, the sadness, the pain, and the pleasure. It can take us on a journey inward or propel us into heroic action!

Breath urges the body to **move**, bringing us to the second lifeline. Stretching, bending, twisting, walking, running, climbing, are natural extensions of breathing. As the body expands and then releases, we find a place to rest - the breath, body, and mind quiet, waiting until stillness arrives.

Stillness gives rise to **mindfulness**, the third lifeline, which, in turn, invites meditation. Arriving at the still and sacred space within us brings a sense of deep peace, infinite joy, and unconditional love. It is here we sense our true nature which is infinite, eternal, and whole. Our true nature is divine essence dwelling within us.

Finding Balance is a resource for those who are struggling with uncertainty and change. It provides tools to create space around whatever it is you are facing and breathe new life and possibility into it. I hope you will read this book with an open mind and heart and find that inner peace within you.

PROLOGUE

Over the past few years I began noticing an alarming trend. My students were coming to class with heavy hearts and similar stories of shifting family dynamics, aging, loss, uncertainty and change.

Our Yoga community falls primarily into the young of heart and mind category so it is reasonable to assume that we would face challenges typical for the Baby Boomer generation. The problem is, we failed to notice that we were aging along with our parents, spouses, friends, children, grandchildren, and the general world around us.

The rude awaking began when Margo, one of our most active 80+ members, was diagnosed with cancer. I visited her once a week in her home to practice yoga that complemented her treatment. Margo recovered and enjoyed a few more healthy years until last fall when she past from complications following heart surgery. Then, Linda, developed kidney failure after the sudden death of her husband. Being a student of yoga for over 50 years, she drew on her well of knowledge, family, and community support to heal and move on. Several women were faced with the reality of care taking their aging parents who were suffering from Alzheimer's or dementia. Another, Connie, welcomed a severely handicapped granddaughter who will require round the clock care for her entire precious life. The list goes on, including Peggy, longtime student who suffered a stroke in class. She was rushed to the hospital and survived with minimal nerve damage to her right side. Peggy continues to practice yoga as we explore modifications that will open up pathways to this new body experience. Others were experiencing loss of friends that were moving away to be with family or simply dying. Lives seemed to be falling apart faster than we could put them back together.

However, in all these cases my students confided that the lifelines they learned in yoga were valuable tools in helping them move through these difficult situations.

The breath, the body and the mind all converge equally to calm, balance, and focus our energy. As we move through each chapter you will find several options for engaging these areas.

The breath elicits a physical response via movement or pose. From the physical form or movement, space opens up for mindfulness and awareness where, you may discover that inner resource from which everything arises: infinite, eternal, and whole.

By the end of this book you will have the resources to manage most emergency situations that you may find yourself facing.

Let's begin by answering a few questions:

1. What is causing uncertainty in your life at the moment?
2. How is this uncertainty manifesting in your body/mind?

Physically_____

Mentally _____

Emotionally_____

Behaviorally_____

On a scale of 1-10, how would you rate your state of "unease" right now? _____

As we progress through the chapters you can revisit these questions and note any changes that are occurring.

CHAPTER 1

BREATH AWARENESS

There are two graces in breathing: drawing in air and
discharging it. The former constrains, the latter refreshes;
so marvelously is life mixed. Thank God then when he
presses you, and thank him again when he lets you go.
Johann Wolfgang von Goethe (1749–1832)

Our first lifeline to finding balance is breath. "Take a deep breath and count to ten" is a familiar phrase used in every culture. Breath is our constant companion from birth to death. Think about it: When we are born, what is the first thing we do? We inhale. What is the last thing we do when leaving our bodies? We exhale. In between, the breath accompanies us every moment. You may consider each inhale a rebirth into this life and each exhale a mini death to the past.

Let's Breathe:

Follow the breath as it flows in and out of the nostrils. What do you notice? Do you feel sensation as the breath moves in and out? Where do you feel the breath in your body? In your chest (shallow), ribs (middle), or belly (deep)?

Compare your inhale to your exhale. Is the inhale longer than the exhale or vice versa? Or are they equal in length? What is easier: to inhale or to exhale?

You can learn a lot about yourself by watching your breath. For instance, if you feel your breath primarily in your chest, this can be a sign you are not fully grounded or in your body. You are in your head, so to speak. This can happen when we are reading, studying, practicing any form of artistic expression, or mentally focused on something for an extended period of time, like watching TV or being connected to any device (computer, phone, tablet). Shallow breathing can also be a symptom of anxiety, worry, and inability to focus. Shallow breathing can make us accident-prone.

On the other hand, if you can feel your breath deep in your belly, you are probably more grounded in your body. This is common when physical exercise is required: working construction, gardening, playing sports, and working out. However, it can also show up in relaxation, sleep, laziness, stubbornness, and devotion.

In Yoga, we often divide the breath into three parts: belly, ribs, chest. To practice breathing, place your hands on your belly and begin to breathe down into the space until you feel your hands moving out with the expansion of your belly. Try to resist any temptation to forcefully push the belly out; instead, just let the breath (the diaphragm pushing down, causing the belly to move out) do the work. As you exhale, your hands will simply follow the belly back inward.

After practicing the "belly breath" for a couple minutes, we move on to the "two part-breath" by adding the rib cage.

While keeping one hand on your belly, bring the other hand to your rib cage, either side. Feel your ribs, if possible, but don't squeeze. Now inhale. The hand on your belly receives the first part of the breath; as you continue to inhale, feel the breath pressing the ribs outward under your other hand. In the beginning, you may want to exaggerate the outward movement of the ribs until you get the feel of it. As you exhale, your ribs will move back inward and your belly will soften. This is the two-part breath. Practice several times before moving on.

The three-part breath adds the chest into the sequence. If you'd like, you can move either hand to the chest or just leave it open and see how it feels. Begin slowly inhaling into your belly, then your ribs, and your chest. Hold a moment, then exhale. Feel your chest falling, ribs narrowing, belly softening. Hold out a moment, then begin again. Repeat at least three times.

This breath helps distribute your breath equally, balancing the energy flow throughout your core and limbs. You may notice resistance to different parts of the breath. This is your indicator light going on. Pay attention, and investigate what's happening, mentally, physically, or emotionally. Our breath is our teacher, our first aide, our friend, and our counselor.

It was a quiet, Sunday morning as I drove north on I-5. Traffic was light, and I was relaxed, when I witnessed a car come tumbling across the road in front of me. It rolled to the median, and without thinking, I pulled over to the side of the road, got out and walked over to the young woman who exited the crashed vehicle. She was in shock. With my arm around her, we made our way to the side of the road, and I sat her down. By now others had stopped and were calling 9-1-1 and directing traffic. Meanwhile, I had begun a practice called "heart to hara breath" with the woman. I placed my right hand at the center of her back and the middle and ring finger of my left hand on her sternum (heart chakra). I instructed her to place her hands over her belly and breathe into her hands, look at her hands, focus on her belly and hands, all while I continued to breathe calmness and peace into her heart center. Bringing her energy down ... grounding it back into her body, into the earth. Time stopped, her breathing slowed, and she became more calm and stable. By now the EMTs were arriving, so I left my charge with a blessing and a prayer.

It has been a few years since then, and I had never shared this story until last fall when I was teaching the course that accompanies this book. The story is an example of why I teach: To know what you know by heart. To allow the "other self" to take over when there is urgent need. To let something bigger than ego take over and do what is needed in the moment.

To practice breathing is to live and give. The inhale is "inspiring" and the exhale is "exhilarating." The inhale brings in life; the exhale takes it away. Simple, but not easy.

As you stay present with your breath, you may notice it changing—lengthening—deepening—slowing down—calming the nervous system—finding more space inside to move and explore. Filling your legs, arms, hand, and feet with breath; your torso, front and back, your neck and head, front and back—your entire body breathing itself.

Practice

Heart to Hara

- Place your right hand over your hara (the energy center just below the navel) and left hand over your heart.
- Inhale into your hara. Feel your belly expand under your hand. Exhale up to your heart. Feel the breath travel up to the heart under your left hand (receiving).
- Inhale back down to your hara.
- Exhale up to your heart.
- Continue this pattern until you feel calm.

This pranayama brings energy and focus out of the head and down into the body. Grounding.

Counting Breaths

- Begin counting backwards from twenty-one to one.
- Inhale twenty-one. Exhale twenty-one.
- Inhale twenty. Exhale twenty. If you lose count, go back to twenty-one and begin again. The object is not to get to zero but to stay focused.

This pranayama helps slow the breath and calm the nervous system. Counting up energizes, and counting down relaxes. Focus. Try this exercise to help fall asleep.

Box Breathing

- Visualize a box or square and inhale to the count of two.
- Hold to the count of two.
- Exhale to the count of two.
- Hold out to the count of two.

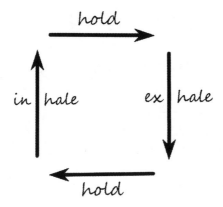

Repeat, increasing the count by one each round until you notice one side is stressed. Stay with this count until the weak side is at ease.

This pranayama brings the mind/body back into balance. Try it when you're caught up in an emotion or thought pattern or just at a loss of what to do.

CHAPTER 2

BODY AWARENESS

Stress is wanting things to be the way they are not.
Michael Lee

By engaging the breath we begin to feel into our body and we therefore access the second lifeline to finding balance: body awareness. This may be an organic response, such as noticing sensation moving down our legs into our feet and toes, or a sensation in the chest spreading out into our shoulders, down our arms, and into our hands and fingers. The urge to stretch, wiggle, or walk are all signs of returning to the body.

One day, after an energy-healing session with my teacher, I began experiencing an intense energy flow up my body and out the crown of my head. It felt like I was literally leaving my body, and I couldn't stop it. My teacher, who was walking next to me said, "Go to your feet. Take your mind and energy to your feet." I obeyed and stayed focused on my feet with a mantra that was simply *feet, feet, feet*. The energy flow began to slow and reverse. We continued walking, me chanting, and after several minutes balance was restored.

Now this example, after the fact, appears like a no-brainer. If you are feeling one way, find it's opposite and feel that. Sometimes we forget we are in charge of our minds and not the other way around.

When you feel the need to reconnect to the earth, there are a few simple actions that you can take. Get dirty. Go outside and dig in the dirt or sand with your hands. Walk barefoot in mud, grass, or sand. Feel nature in its raw form. Go to a body of water and wade. Go to the forest and hike. Go to a park and enjoy being outside. Get active and go tech free for a time.

In nature, we experience an energy exchange that is lacking when we only interact with technology and machines. Human beings were created to live in a natural world, not an artificial one.

The following exercises and poses are commonly found in Qigong and Yoga. They are easy and are especially helpful in guiding you back to your body/mind.

Chalas:

- Foot circles - lubricating the joints in the toes, feet, & ankles
- Knee circles
- Hip circles
- Swing twist
- Shoulder rolls

- Arm and wrist circles
- Neck and head circles
- Sarpa - meaning the serpent done in a spinal wave movement.

Reference video on YouTube:
https://www.youtube.com/watch?v=bgh12tj75F4

Six Movements of the Spine

1. Flex and extension (forward bend and back bend)

- *Dog tail / Cat back* - begin on your hands and knees (table pose)
- Inhale - look forward and relax the back (tail in the air)
- Exhale - arch the spine upwards (cat back)

2. Lateral bending left and right

- Standing or sitting, bring your arms up over head or to the hips;
- Inhale, lengthen, exhale, bend to right
- Inhale up, lengthen, exhale, bend to left
- Inhale up, lengthen and repeat two more times

3. Twist or spiral left and right

- Sit on a chair (legs together) or cross-legged on the floor;
- Bring your right hand to your left knee and place your left hand behind you.
- Inhale, lengthen,

- Exhale, begin to take your navel to the left, followed by your chest, then your nose, pause as you inhale and then continue into the twist by gently pressing the palm of your right hand into the outside of your left knee, resist.
- Inhale, lengthen,
- Exhale unwind back to neutral.
- Repeat to the other side. Taking three breaths in each twist.

4. Child's Pose

- Kneel with your forehead to the floor or a prop (blanket, pillow or block) if needed.
- Your back is rounded, arms to the sides or hands under your forehead.
- The most important thing is to have your back slightly rounded so you can receive breath into it easily.
- If your hips don't reach your heels, place a blanket between them.
- In this position, take three to six breaths.
- Toes can turn under or point back, whatever is most comfortable.

5. Crocodile

- Lie face down with your hands under your forehead and elbows pointing out.
- Gently rock your hips back and forth allowing the hips, sacrum and lower back to release.

6. Half Frog

- Lie face down, turn your left cheek to the floor, place your left arm down by your side, and your right arm and hand up by your face.
- Right leg bends out to your side no higher than the hip.
- Remain in your pose for a least 6 breaths.
- Slowly come back to crocodile before moving to the other side.
- You may want to use a blanket if there is discomfort anywhere in this pose.

All these choices give the body an opportunity to ground itself. Facing the earth, we naturally begin to feel comforted, calmer, and at ease. You notice the breath pushing against the ground sending a signal to the body/mind that you are supported and safe.

CHAPTER 3

MINDFULNESS

I could be hostage to my ego or host to God.
Marianne Williamson

Once you have engaged the breath and grounded through movement and body awareness, the third lifeline opens up through mindfulness.

Mindfulness is a popular term these days. You see it popping up on the news and in magazines. Books devoted to mindfulness abound online and in bookstores. There are classes that will teach you mindfulness techniques, but what is it exactly?

Mindfulness is: To be awake, alert aware and present to what's happening now.

Mindfulness can slip into meditation very easily. This happens when you begin practicing a mindfulness technique that elicits a spacious awareness within you. This can also be perceived as a loving presence or a sacred place connecting you to your higher spiritual power.

There are many mindfulness practices to choose from and one size does not fit all so you will need to try several to find which one works best for you. An easy place to start is to sit comfortably on the floor or in a chair, place your hands palms up, eyes open or closed, and watch the breath flow in and out.

If you have an active or restless mind you may want to start with a mantra meditation, where you repeat a phrase or word. Some people don't care to sit still so they may choose a walking meditation. Others may not be able to stay focused with their eyes closed, so they practice an open eye meditation (tratak), gazing at a fixed object like a candle or flower.

Mindfulness is paramount to finding balance and clarity in uncertain times - one moment at a time. The breath leads us to the next moment, and so on until we find our way back to a sense of peace and equilibrium.

Let's try **Mantra:**

Pick a word or phrase that has meaning for you. Maybe think; peace, om, love, or thy will be done, may I be happy, may I be peaceful. Remember to keep it short. As you become comfortable, begin to breathe. Listening to the sound of your breath you will begin to notice the mantra merging with your breath.

Begin by repeating the mantra out loud. It will sometimes take on a pleasant rhythm or tone. It is also okay to sing the mantra. As you continue, there may come a time when the mantra naturally turns inward. The idea is to plant the mantra in the background of your mind so it is always with you.

Walking meditation:

Walking meditation is just what it sounds like. Walk slowly and focus on how your feet are connecting to the ground. Heel to toe. Pay attention as the weight shifts from one leg/foot to the other, remembering to always stay present. Walk and feel the energy of what's surrounding you. Walk and chant your mantra. Walk and watch your breath. Walk and listen - be aware, feel the rhythm of movement. Walk as long as you like.

Eyes Open (tratak):

Choose an object. Popular choices are: a candle, a flower, a yantra or mandala, a simple picture, a tree, the ocean. We will use a candle for this practice.

Make yourself comfortable in a chair or on the floor. Position your candle at eye level or wherever you can fix your gaze without creating stress in your neck, upper back and shoulders.

Begin by experiencing your breath while gazing at the candle. As the breath quiets, your attention shifts solely to the candle. Let your eyes soften -there is no effort required for this practice. Just watch and let your mind become absorbed by the flame. Don't worry, you can blink.

Your mindfulness practice could last 5 minutes or for hours. Remember, some time is better than no time.

CHAPTER 4

YOUR INNER RESOURCE

Be still and know that I AM God.
Psalm 46:10

What we are looking for is what is looking.
St. Francis of Assisi

How do we get to *this* place? Well, you are on the path if you have been using the lifelines of breath awareness, body awareness, and mindfulness. This path is ancient and has been travelled by many masters, saints, and devotees. It is because of those who have paved the way, that we can follow in their footsteps. Cultivating your practice leads to insights along the way. These insights are usually personal and speak to your unique life path or dharma.

There will come times when you need a rest. This next lifeline is called your inner resource. Your inner resource is a place where you feel safe, comforted, and loved. Close your eyes and think of a time when you felt completely safe, comforted, and loved. It can be anywhere: a room, a beach, a mountain, a porch swing with grandma. Choose one for now and recreate the scene including: people, animals, surroundings, smells, sounds, feelings, and emotions, related to the place. It is important to embody the feelings and emotions that this environment offers.

Once you have found this inner resource, know you can visit it anytime to take a break or a mini retreat. Feel free to have several versions to address your needs.

Another inner resource is the central channel, sometimes also referred to as the river of life (for this text we will use the former and abbreviate as CC). This resource is more physical and grounding so you can use it when you need to get back in touch with your body. Below are a couple practices that will help you experience this place when you feel ready.

First, find the central channel. The CC is located in front of the spine and runs through the chakras (energy centers) channeling prana (life force energy) through your body and between heaven and earth.

Visualize the breath as it flows in through your nostrils and down into the central channel (CC) through the chakras, and into earth below. As you exhale, visualize the breath flowing back up from the earth, through the CC and out the crown of your head (not the nostrils). Next inhale, visualize the breath entering the CC through the crown and down the channel back to earth. Continue this practice until you begin to feel the flow of prana as well as breath. Prana travels with breath.

(Feel free to record the following practice. Some may find it easier to follow directions if they are spoken.)

Second, we can use the central channel as our center when we want to feel balanced, steady, and sure.

Stand (or sit) with your eyes closed or open and visualize the prana flowing through the CC. Slowly begin to shift your awareness into the back of your body: heels, calves, back of the knees, hamstrings, buttocks, sacrum, spine, shoulder blades, back of the arms, triceps, elbows, little fingers, back of the neck and head. Be in the back of your body, feel it expand beyond physical form. Take a deep breath into the back and exhale back to the CC. Be in the CC, the river of life.

Begin to shift your awareness into the front of your body: toes, tops of the feet, ankles, shin bones, knee caps, quads, pelvis, front of the torso, chest, shoulders, biceps, front of the elbows, thumbs and index fingers, notch at the base of your throat, front of the neck and face. Breathe into the entire front of your body and extend your awareness beyond physical form. Take a deep breath into the front of your body and exhale back to the CC. Breathe. Be in the river of life.

Slowly begin to shift your awareness into the left side of your body. Breathe into the left foot, leg, hip (front and back), left side of the torso, left arm, hand and fingers, left side of the neck (front and back), face and head. Expand beyond the physical into the space on the left side of your body. Take a breath in and exhale back into the CC.

Be in the CC, the river of life. Take a breath and move into the right side of your body. Breath into the right foot, leg, hip, torso (front and back), right shoulder, arm, hand and fingers, right side of the neck, face and head. Breathe into the right side of the body and into the space beyond. Inhale and exhale back to the CC.

Be here and experience the front, back, left, and right sides, while, simultaneously, remaining in the CC. Feel the space surrounding you: above, below, out front, behind, to the left and to the right - feel your aura (energy field) radiating.

With practice you'll be able to do this in a few seconds, all while holding your center calm and relaxed. This is helpful to do before balancing poses in yoga or when you need to get out of your head and back into your body.

CHAPTER 5

THE "I AM" PRESENCE

The Tao that can be talked about is not the true Tao.
The name that can be named is not the eternal Tao.
The Tao Te Ching I

During the course of practice there may come a time when you experience something indescribable. Something so special it takes your breath away or blows your mind. These are YOUR moments of enlightenment, YOUR moments of truth and YOUR moments of knowing that you know, no doubt, no questioning.

Cherish these gifts. Keep them close. Don't try to share these gifts because they can't be shared. They are indescribable. Take some time to reflect on your experience and journal if you'd like. This is personal, intimate, wisdom unique to your life.

Unlike a dream, these moments are imprinted in your body/ mind. They remain imbedded within you. During yoga or meditation you may recall your truth but remembering is not the same as experiencing.

Remembering takes you into the past. Experiencing keeps us in the present. Expectation springs you forward into the future. Staying present is the key to any practice. There is always something waiting to distract us.

Sometimes life unexpectedly delivers you an experience from out of nowhere. "Didn't see that one coming." Or "What just happened?" This is the universe waking you up ... often referred to as the "wakeup call".

This "wakeup call" has happened to me a few times. It is kind of a short-cut to enlightenment that you didn't ask for. This is one of mine:

Once upon a time, I exercised race horses at various tracks across the U.S. and abroad. Needless to say, there were times that either myself or others around me were riding horses that chose to not behave. One of those days happened to be at Detroit Race Course (DRC). I had ridden this particular horse before and knew she was skittish, nervous, and unpredictable. We entered the track along with maybe 30 other horses out for morning workouts. The first lap went well and we had relaxed into a gentle gallop when suddenly my mount just stopped. I flipped off to the left and my boot got hung up in the stirrup. I was left hanging upside down.

While horses galloped by on both sides, my horse stood dead still. Instantly I knew that if she took one step my leg would break or my head could be bashed in - neither were good scenarios. That's when it happened. My life passed before my eyes. I'd heard about this phenomenon but didn't understand how it could be possible. Now I knew. It was like time stood still and I had all the time in the world to look and see my life all at once, not in chronological order but a multidimensional experience. It was fascinating. Then, it was over.

An outrider rescued me before my horse decided to make a move. A miracle to this day that I thank God for. My trainer rode up and yelled at me for performing circus tricks on the track. Not funny. By then the adrenaline had kicked in and I realized I had just dodged a huge bullet and been given a priceless gift simultaneously.

This wakeup call created a profound paradigm shift within me, one that has informed the years since in shaping and guiding me along my journey.

Why share this story and not the ones that come through meditation? The "wakeup call" happens to most of us at least once in our lives. We are not cultivating it, we aren't seeking, we are just living. These experiences can be shared if they can benefit the "other".

I hope you will find the lifelines in this book useful when you are facing uncertain times or just need to get back in touch with yourself. If you would like to share your thoughts or experiences pertaining to the practices given in this book, please contact me: Nancy@bodyawarenessyoga.com. I look forward to hearing from you.

Until then, may you be happy, may you be peaceful, and may you live with ease.

CHAPTER 6

UNCERTAIN TIMES: COVID – 19

When I began writing this book I had no idea it would take three years to complete. Now, after an intense year of caretaking my, still in hospice, father and witnessing my once vibrant young at heart mother dissolve into an old woman before my eyes, Covid-19 has arrived.

This is a new chapter in world history and life as we know- or knew - is no more. The paradigm has shifted and we must begin to make peace with this change and perhaps this new normal. The difference with Covid-19 is that it is the collective rather than individual experience that is fueling the fire. The impact is intensified or diversified depending on how you process energy. If you are sensitive to the energy of others, your experience may be amplified. On the other hand, if you are less affected by the energy of others, your personal experience may be less intense. We tend to attract "like" energy and repel "opposite". This may be useful to remember when interacting with others during these difficult times. We all process change differently and there are no exact rules. Be patient and compassionate to one another.

In this final chapter I discuss how to integrate what we already know into a practice of balancing the collective energy of this pandemic. It is no longer *just* us, this is a global crisis that demands our attention and intention to create a space for something new to emerge.

We will practice breath for denial; movement for anger and depression; and mindfulness for bargaining and acceptance. You may recognize the five stages of grief, which I've chosen to help us navigate this novel time in history. The stages of grief are not in any order, nor does everyone necessarily experience all of them. This pandemic is turning out to be a literal and figurative dying of life as we knew it as well as a birth of a new way of being. It is my hope that these stages will be helpful to give structure to our recovery process.

Let's take a deep breath. Inhale through the nose and exhale though the mouth letting go of the breath. Do this several times while you visualize gathering up thoughts, feelings, and emotions you'd like to let go of and then on the exhale actually let them go… whoosh. Close your eyes and begin to breathe through the nostrils, in and out. Where's your breath? Is it in your chest? Is it in your ribs? Is it in your belly? Is it in all three? Keep watching your breath until it becomes deep and long. This may take a while but be patient. Enjoy being with your breath.

Now that we've centered, let's begin with the obvious stage of grief, **denial**. When we look at denial, it doesn't stand alone. Denial has friends: shock, fear, confusion, avoidance, and the list could go on and on. These all are states of mind. When you are in denial it is really your mind that has been hijacked. You are stuck in your head or in other words, the elements of air and space make "vata" its nature. The body is absent. You are experiencing an out of body experience.

As we learned in Chapter one, the first lifeline is the breath and we use it to ground ourselves back to our body. We need to get grounded gently so we begin to breathe into the belly. Place a hand on your belly and feel it expand with the in breath and soften as you exhale out. This breath will continue to help draw your attention down into your body helping to calm your mind. Once your mind has slowed down a bit, you may want to try the Hara to Heart breath (Ref. Chpt 1). When you feel ready, and if possible, go outside in your garden or to a park. Nature is an excellent partner in bringing us back to what is real. Students who helped me workshop this chapter mentioned that their pets were a source of great comfort and helped to ground them.

When you practice yoga during this stage of denial, choose poses that are comforting and quiet like child's pose, half frog, or crocodile. These poses all face toward the ground, get it? Grounding poses. Avoid poses that involve vigorous movement causing more agitation of air and space (vata) (Ref. Chpt 2). Finally, try a slow walking meditation focusing attention on your feet, barefoot if possible. Stay present - no past, no future, just NOW (Ref. Chpt. 3).

The second stage of grief is **anger.** Like denial, anger has friends: frustration, irritation, anxiety, resistance, fight and many more. Anger is an emotion that has the elements of fire and air making "Pitta" its nature. Anger wants to be expressed and we need to help direct it in a positive way that does no harm. The breath once again begins this engagement with what is known as breath of joy (or Life). While standing, pretend you are the conductor of an orchestra or band. With a sniffing breath begin to raise your arms out in front while sniffing 1/3 breath into the belly. Your arms then sweep out wide to the sides while sniffing another 1/3 breath into the ribs, then sweep the arms above your head as you fill your chest completing the breath. Now release both arms down towards the ground, along with your body, while exhaling out the mouth with a loud "HA"(like the sound you would make if karate chopping a block of wood). As you rise up, arms fly up in front again beginning the next round. Repeat several times but be careful not to make yourself light headed.

Another breath to try is the wood chopper. Pretend you are holding a medium size ax with both hands. Inhale the ax overhead and as you release the ax down to chop the wood let out a loud "HA". Don't forget to bend your knees when the ax drops, you'll get a good leg workout. This feels great and allows clarity to arrive with possibilities of where to direct this transformed energy. During your yoga practice try sun salutations and then the warrior series (I & II). For your mindfulness practice, go outside and jog/walk fast, or take a challenging hike. Remember, anger energy needs to be engaged and directed in a positive direction.

Bargaining is the third stage of grief. Remember, there is no order to these stages and some may not be experienced at all. Bargaining has friends that are more complicated. We find ourselves back in the head trying to make sense of the situation (vata). We begin to reach out to others by telling our story and listening to theirs. We begin to weave together a new narrative, maybe toying with the idea that if "I do this, then I can change that." This is good news. By creating new scenarios that are acceptable options, you figure out how to manifest them, leading you towards a new vision for your life. To help you find your way, we will focus on balance during yoga practice. The breath we use is box breathing (Ref. Chpt. 1). The other breath or pranayama I would recommend is alternate nostril breathing (nadi shodhna). This is practiced by inhaling in one nostril, exhaling out the other, inhaling in the later, exhaling out the former and continued for several rounds. Use a thumb to gently hold one nostril closed as you inhale, then release it when time to exhale. Repeat in the opposite direction.

For asana practice, do your chalas and then try balancing poses like tree and airplane, then move to lateral poses either standing or on the floor. To end your practice, find a yoga nidra recording to play. You can easily find these online at Insight Meditation or i-Rest (Richard Miller, Phd.). CD's are available if you still use a CD player.

Depression is the fourth stage of grief and can easily slip under the radar if we are not vigilant. Feeling overwhelmed, helpless, lonely, sad, hostile, or heavy are all evidence of the earth element, "Kapha". The first thing humans are prone to do is seek comfort and safety: stay home, stay safe, save lives. Done. The longer we stay home and seek comfort and safety you may begin to add food for comfort, TV for entertainment, and sleep (or another inert activity) instead of exercise. Before you know it you've gained five pounds and are starting to feel crummy, useless, helpless and not in control. Time to WAKE UP!

This takes us back to the practice of breath of joy we used with anger. We need to move that stagnant energy and recharge your battery. Jumping, bouncing, or shaking are other easy standing options. Breathe! Bring your hands to your shoulders and pull your elbows back while squeezing your shoulder blades together. Inhale. As you exhale, bring your elbows forward and together in front of your chest. Then, inhale expand, elbows out and back, exhale, contract elbows forward and together. Do this at least three to six times. This is called expanded chest breathing and is part of the heart opening process.

Depression is a contraction of body, mind, & spirit so we need to focus on expanding by opening up the body again to let life back in and get it flowing. For your yoga practice we look to back bends, standing poses, and inversions. Inversions can be any pose that elevates your hips higher than your heart. Try practicing bridge, whale, half bow, full bow, boat, or camel. If you are not familiar with any of these poses, simply lie down near a wall and put your legs up. To create an inversion you can place a pillow or blanket under your hips while your legs are up the wall. Let your arms rest out to your sides palms up. Your mindfulness practice can be walking or open-eyed meditation. Also, to counter depression, it is helpful to keep your eyes open during practice.

This limits any opportunity to slip back into sloth and torpor (I love that word).

At some point, sooner or later, we arrive at **acceptance** and peace. We have come to a place where we are mentally, physically, emotionally, and spiritually engaged (tridosha). We are actively exploring options, reflecting and reconstructing a vision, making plans, and beginning to take action. A new routine is emerging and we are feeling more empowered. We have some control in our lives and over our circumstances. When we are in this wonderful place, our breath is choice. Our yoga practice and movement are choice. Our mindfulness practice is choice.

What do you need today? Whatever you want. Try something new. Make it fun. Enjoy this feeling of hope and joy. Anything is possible. It is my hope that acceptance and peace show up during the course of each day at least once. Remember these moments when you begin to feel sad or angry. They will help bring you back into balance.

We are all in this together and together we will make our way out. There will be different paths for us but as long as we are kind and patient with one another we can successfully transition through these uncertain times.

ABOUT THE AUTHOR

Nancy Sanks founded Body Awareness Yoga in 1989. Located in San Diego, Ca., she has served the community for over thirty years. Offering classes, retreats, workshops, and special guests, she and her students have grown within this loving and supportive community.

Kripalu Center for Yoga and Health is located in West Stockbridge, Mass and is where Nancy has received advanced training in Yoga, Ayurveda, i-Rest, and Phoenix Rising Yoga Therapy. She also has studied extensively with Angela Farmer and Rama Jyoti Vernon.

Married forty years with four children, nine grandchildren, and elderly parents nearby, Nancy is busy living a full life. She is now beginning to put her practice into writing.

With this first book, Finding Balance in Uncertain Times, she hopes to reach students that want to take their practice to the next level. Making the teachings of yoga available to anyone with a desire to embody lovingkindness and a healthy lifestyle is what motivates Nancy to get up and keep going every day.

SUGGESTED READING

The Healing Path of Yoga, by Nischala Joy Devi; Three Rivers Press, New York

Yoga for Depression, by Amy Weintraub; Broadway Books

Ayurveda for Your Mind, by Janesh Vaidya; Life Publications

Yoga, The Practice of Myth & Sacred Geometry, by Rama Jyoti Vernon; Lotus Press ;

Ageless Soul by Thomas Moore; St. Martin's Press

Still Here, by Ram Dass; Riverhead Books, The Berkley Publishing Group

Seeds of Contemplation, by Thomas Merton; A New Directions Book published by James Laughlin

Seeds, by Thomas Merton selected and edited by Robert Inchausti; Shambhala Publications, Inc

The Tao of Inner Peace, by Diane Dreher; Penguin Group, Penguin Putnam Inc.

Siddhartha, Hermann Hesse; A New Directions Book published by New Directions Publishing Corporation

Hildegard of Bingen, A Saint for our Times, by Matthew Fox; Namaste Publishing

The Great Work of Your Life, by Stephen Cope; Bantam Books

Loving-Kindness, the Revolutionary Art of Happiness, by Sharon Salzberg; Shambhala Publications, Inc.

The Tao Te Ching, by Lao Tzu

Practicing Peace in Times of War, by Pema Chodron; Shambhala Publishing, Inc.

The Book of Joy, Lasting Happiness in a Changing World, by His Holiness the Dalai Lama and Achbishop Desmond Tutu with Douglas Abrams; AVERY an imprint of Penguin Random House

Creative Visualization, by Shakti Gwain; Bantam New Age Books

Seeking Peace, by Mary Pipher, Riverhead Books

The Green Boat, by Mary Pipher, Riverhead Books

Women Rowing North, by Mary Pipher; Bloomsbury Publishing

Honoring the Medicine, the Essential Guide to Native American Healing, by Kenneth Cohen; Ballentine Books

Grandmothers Counsel the World, Women Elders Offer Their Vision for Our Planet, by Carol Schaefer; Trumpeter Books an imprint of Shambhala Publications, Inc

ACKNOWLEDGEMENTS

T hank you Michelle Murphy and Joanna Guild my daughters and co-editors. Without you I may have given up and never finished this project.

Thank you Body Awareness Yoga community for your support and feedback throughout these past thirty years. It is because of you that I continue to learn, grow, and teach.

Words cannot express my gratitude to all the teachers who shared their knowledge and wisdom with me throughout the years. This includes the entire faculty of The Kripalu Center for Yoga and Health, Kripalu School of Ayurveda, Phoenix Rising Yoga Therapy, Richard Miller, PhD., Integrative Restoration-iRest, Janesh Vaidya, Ayurveda Practitioner, and master teachers, Angela Farmer, and Rama Jyoti Vernon. These represent just a sample of the deep roots I draw from.

Finally, I'd like to thank God, the Grandmothers and Grandfathers of all tribes and nations, teachers of this life and past, who guide me daily and remind me that I am just a vessel channeling unconditional love.

Printed in the United States
By Bookmasters